£6.99

Welcome!

Hey there Scooby fans!

Welcome to the Scooby-Doo! Annual 2005! This is the place to get the lowdown on everyone's favourite goofy Great Dane and his crime-crunching sidekicks.

Every page is packed with mystery, monsters and scooberific adventures. So hop on board The Mystery Machine and join Scooby and the gang for gruesome giggles, spooky stories and a howling good time ... that's if you're brave enough! Scooby-dooby-doo!

SCOOBY-DOO! ™

Contents

DAN ABNETT   Writer
ANTHONY WILLIAMS   Penciller
DAN DAVIS   Inker
JENNA GARCIA & GUSTAV   Letterers
PAUL BECTON   Colorist
DIGITAL CHAMELEON   Separations
HARVEY RICHARDS   Asst Editor
JOAN HILTY   Editor

CONTINUED ON PAGE 12

9

MEET THE GANG!

Say hello to Scooby-Doo and the gang, and get the lowdown on the grooviest supersleuths around!

SCOOBY

Name: Scoobert
Nickname: Scooby-Doo, Scooby, Scoob - he answers to them all!
Age: 7
Scooby style: A goofy Great Dane with a furry brown coat and a groovy blue dog collar.
Likes: Scooby Snacks! This hound loves nothing more than chowing down with a big feast of tasty treats!
Dislikes: Ghosts, ghouls and feeling hungry!
Favourite phrase: "Rooby-rooby-roo!"
Fact: If a spook appears while Scooby is snoozing, his ears will tap him on the head to wake him up!

'Rooby-rooby

Shaggy

Name: Norville Rogers
Nickname: Shaggy
Age: 17
Scooby style: A groovy dude with a crazy mop of hair which gave him his nickname.

Likes: Just like Scooby, Shaggy loves to snack!
Dislikes: Monsters!
Favourite phrase: "Zoinks!"
Fact: Nobody can escape quicker than Shaggy when he is running from a ghost! He's even been known to use roller skates to make a totally speedy getaway!

THE MYSTERY MACHINE

The Mystery Machine is an important member of the Mystery, Inc. gang! It has a top speed of 60 MPH and it has a room in the back for a computer, a built-in radar and even a photography dark room!

FRED

Name: Fred Jones
Nickname: Freddy
Age: 16
Scooby style: Fred is known for being calm and sensible. His trademark look is his orange Ascot tie.
Likes: As the leader of the gang, Fred loves being in charge.
Dislikes: Being outwitted by a monster
Favourite phrase: "Well, that wraps up this mystery!"
Fact: Fred is an amateur inventor who loves creating crazy gizmos and monster traps.

DAPHNE

Name: Daphne Blake
Nickname: Danger Prone Daphne
Age: 16
Scooby style: Daphne loves to look good! She wears a groovy purple dress with matching hairband.
Likes: Solving mysteries
Dislikes: Falling through trap doors
Favourite phrase: "Jeepers!"
Fact: Daphne's father bought the Mystery Machine for the gang.

VELMA

Name: Velma Dinkley
Nickname: Doesn't have one
Age: 15
Scooby style: A science geek! Velma wears an orange jumper, red skirt and black glasses.
Likes: Using her immense brain power to unmuddle mysteries.
Dislikes: Missing a vital clue
Favourite phrase: "Jinkies"
Fact: Shaggy knows how often Velma loses her glasses, so he always carries a spare pair for her.

CONTINUED FROM PAGE 9

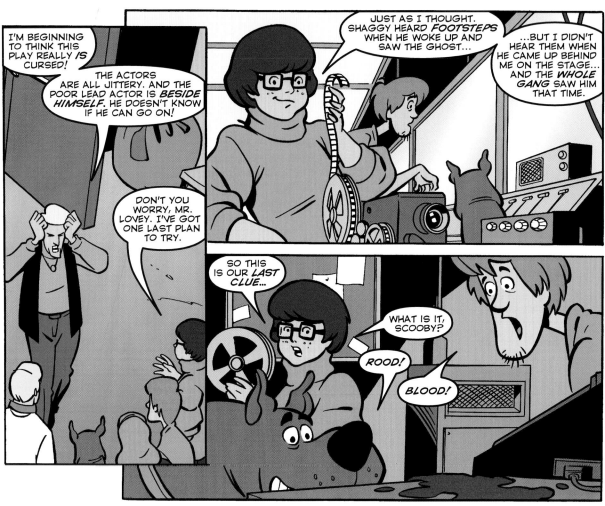

BUT WHO COULD IT BE?

LET'S FIND OUT!

IT'S AN *UNDERSTUDY*... BUT WHY?

AFTER FINDING THE NOTE AND THE DAGGER IN THE *STAR'S* DRESSING ROOM, I'D GUESS HE'S JEALOUS.

YOU MEAN HE WANTED TO PLAY MACBETH SO BADLY THAT HE TRIED TO TERRIFY MY STAR ACTOR?

AND HE NEARLY SCARED AWAY *ALL* MY ACTORS!

BUT HOW DID HE MOVE AROUND SO QUICKLY?

THAT'S THE *CLEVER* PART.

HE MADE A *FILM* OF HIMSELF IN COSTUME AND PROJECTED IT ONTO THE STAGE!

THAT'S WHY WE DIDN'T HEAR HIS *FOOTSTEPS* --AND WHY *YOU* DIDN'T NOTICE THE *COSTUME* WAS MISSING...

...UNTIL *SHAGGY* SAW THE REAL THING WHEN HE USED IT BETWEEN REHEARSALS!

I ONLY WANTED TO BE A STAR... JUST *ONCE*.

WELL, YOU'D BE A STAR IN THE *SPECIAL EFFECTS* DEPARTMENT, BUT NOT BEFORE YOU'VE PUT THIS MESS RIGHT!

LO, THE PERFORMANCE BEGINS...

LIKE, IT'S THE DUDE WITH THE DAGGER AGAIN!

REAH, RAGGY. RHIS IS RARY!

LIKE, DON'T WORRY, SCOOB. THEY DON'T NEED YOUR TONGUE, THEY'VE GOT ONE OF THEIR OWN!

RUH! RUKKY!

AND I'D LIKE TO THANK MY YOUNG FRIENDS HERE FOR MAKING THIS PRODUCTION OF MACBETH POSSIBLE!

LIKE, WHERE'S THE ACTOR IN THE SHAKESPEARE COSTUME?

WHAT? WE DON'T HAVE AN ACTOR PLAYING SHAKESPEARE.

YIKES!

LIKE, MAYBE SHAKESPEARE WANTED TO STOP THE JINX TOO?

ENCORE, SCOOBY! ENCORE!

HA! HA! HA!

THE END

CREEPY CASTLE!

Escape Count Dracula's castle before he and his spooky friends catch you! Play the game with a friend – all you need are counters and a dice!

START!

YOU GET SPOOKED BY A BIG COB WEB. MISS A TURN.
1

2

YOU SAVE DAPHNE FROM A VAMPIRE BAT. GO FORWARD THREE SPACES.
3

7

YOU FIND A CLUE! GO FORWARD ONE SPACE.

6

5 **YOU'VE FORGOTTEN THE SCOOBY SNACKS. GO BACK TO THE START.**

4

8

A GHOST JUMPS OUT AND SCARES YOU. MISS A TURN.
9

10

DRACULA CHASES YOU. RUN TO SPACE 14 AND HIDE!
11

YOU HIDE INSIDE A SUIT OF ARMOUR.
15
MISS A TURN.

14

13 **SCARE THE CREEPY COUNT AWAY WITH SOME GARLIC! TAKE ANOTHER TURN!**

12

16 **FRED WANTS TO MAKE A TRAP. FOLLOW HIM TO THE NEXT SPACE SO YOU CAN HELP.**

17

VELMA LOSES HER GLASSES. MISS A TURN TO HELP HER FIND THEM.
18

FINISH!
WELL DONE! YOU ESCAPED COUNT DRACULA'S CASTLE!

THE FRIGHT BEFORE CHRISTMAS!

FRANK STROM -- writer
JOE STATON -- penciller * DAVE HUNT -- inker
TOM ORZECHOWSKI -- letterer * PAUL BECTON -- colorist
DIGITAL CHAMELEON -- separations

'TWAS THE NIGHT BEFORE THE NIGHT BEFORE CHRISTMAS...

FIVE O'CLOCK AT LAST! HEADING *HOME*, BOB?

ME? ARE YOU KIDDING?

SCROOGE INC.
ACCOUNTING, TAX PREPARATION & LOANS

I'VE STILL GOT *CHRISTMAS SHOPPING* TO DO!

YOU'LL HAVE TO DO IT LATER, CRATCHET -- I NEED YOU TO WORK *OVERTIME!*

CONTINUED ON PAGE 28

Ghost Hunt

Can you help the gang to track down these monsters?
The ghouls are hiding in the grid and you can find them horizontally,
vertically, upwards and downwards.

```
G H O S T C L O W N B
A R L A A B V N E H L
N E B Z L I M L R C A
T P W V I G Y Y E B C
E E I G E F M S W N K
R E T S N O M P O O K
I R C Y L O U Y L T N
P C H M T T M G F E I
M H W N H R H E Z L G
A U A H G O S H R E H
V H D T S V L T N K T
P O L T E R G E I S T
```

CHECK LIST:

- Poltergeist ☐
- Mummy ☐
- Black Knight ☐
- Ghost ☐
- Big Foot ☐
- Witch ☐
- Vampire ☐
- Alien ☐
- The Gypsy ☐
- Skeleton ☐
- Creeper ☐
- Zombie ☐
- Bat ☐
- Werewolf ☐
- Monster ☐
- Phantom ☐
- Ghost Clown ☐

ONE OF THE GOONY GHOULS HAS ESCAPED FROM THE GRID! CAN YOU WORK OUT WHICH ONE IS MISSING?

THE MISSING GHOUL IS ...

PROPERTY OF...
MYSTERY, INC.

Missing ghoul: Zombie

MONSTER MYSTERIES!

Take a look through the Mystery, Inc. case files and discover the facts about some of the most terrifying monsters they have taken on!

HOWL ABOUT THAT?

The gang have tackled a whole host of big, bad werewolves and they are always totally terrifying!

Werewolves are half human, half wolf. They have large white fangs, glowing red eyes and bodies covered in hair. They can run really fast and according to Shaggy, they smell pretty bad too!

OH MUMMY!

Mummification preserved the bodies of Ancient Pharaohs for the afterlife. The body would be washed and wrapped in linen strips and buried... but sometimes they are said to come back to life!

Scooby and the gang have unravelled some mad mummy mysteries! They have been chased by a 2,000 year old mummy and have tackled a moaning mummy who could turn people into stone! Super spooky or what?

DOCTOR, DOCTOR!

Zombies are high up on the Mystery, Inc. list of Most Spooky Spooks! Also known as the Living Dead, these crazy creatures wander around in a ghostlike state causing trouble.

Originating from the island of Haiti, a witch doctor administers a poisonous substance to the victim. They appear to be dead and are buried. Then the witch doctor revives them and they live their life as a ghostly slave. Don't get too spooked, all the zombies the gang have met so far have been phony fakes!

Ghoul Guide!

Do you know your freaky phantoms from your grizzly ghouls? Velma explains the difference between all the different sorts of spooks!

APPARITION

An apparition is a visible ghost you can see, so keep your eyes peeled!

SPIRIT

A floating spook with no body to appear in like other ghosts. They just like to flit about!

POLTERGEIST

An angry spook who loves to make noise, throw dishes around and create chaos. Jeepers, that sounds sorta spooky!

GHOUL

A cheeky ghost who likes to make mischief! They sure do send a shiver down Scooby's spine!

PHANTOM

A phantom appears to be real and they just love to choose a favourite spot for a bit of haunting!

SPOOK SEARCH!

Can you help Fred to trap all these freaky creeps in the word grid? Work out how many letters there are in each word and fit them into the grid.

Werewolf (8)

Spirit (6)

Mummy (5)

Phantom (7)

Poltergeist (11)

Zombie (6)

Ghoul (5)

Apparition (10)

25

HOW TO DRAW SHAGGY!

Follow these easy steps to create your own drawings of the grooviest dude in Coolsville, Shaggy!

1

Follow the steps from 1-4 to draw Shaggy. Follow the steps as closely as you can and use a pencil so that you can rub out any unwanted lines as you go. Start with a sausage shape for his body and a circle for his head.

2

Add two lines for his legs and draw in the shape of his shoes. Draw two lines for the position of his arms and oval shapes for his hands. Now you can draw in Shaggy's mop of hair!

3

Draw in Shaggy's tee shirt and complete his arms and hands. Add the details to his shoes.

4

Add the details to Shaggy's face and head. Draw in his knobbly knees and some shape to Shaggy's tee shirt. Draw over the finished shape in pen and rub out any unwanted lines. Zoinks! Like this should leave you with a totally groovy Shaggy sketch!

LIKE, HEY SCOOB, YOU'RE SUPPOSED TO BE DRAWING *ME!*

Follow these three steps to draw a Shaggy portrait. Start with a circle for his face and a sausage shape for his chin. Sketch in his facial features and his hair and build in the details from there. When you reach step 3, use a pen to draw your final drawing and rub out any unwanted lines.

Now have a go for yourself! Follow the steps to create your own Shaggy picture below!

THAT'S OUR *CUE!* LET'S GET 'IM, GANG!

GREAT PLAN, VELMA! IT'S *FOOLPROOF!*

IT'S *STUCK!*

THE *PLAN?*

NO--THE *DOOR!* WE'RE *TRAPPED!!*

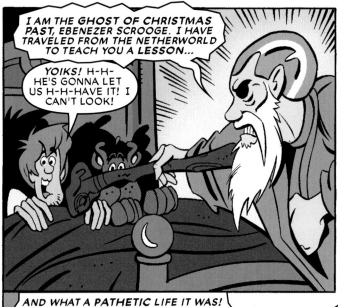

I AM THE GHOST OF CHRISTMAS *PAST,* EBENEZER SCROOGE. I HAVE TRAVELED FROM THE NETHERWORLD TO TEACH YOU A LESSON...

YOIKS! H-H-HE'S GONNA LET US H-H-HAVE IT! I CAN'T LOOK!

ER...WHAT'S WITH, LIKE, THE *PICTURES?*

DON'T YOU *RECOGNIZE* THEM? THEY'RE YOUR *LIFE,* EBENEZER!

AND WHAT A *PATHETIC* LIFE IT WAS! WHILE YOU *SQUANDERED* YOUR TIME PILING UP WEALTH--

--BOB CRATCHET *LIVED,* LOVED, AND PRODUCED A SON, YOUNG TINY TIM. HIS LIFE IS JOYFUL AND *FULFILLING!*

LIKE, HE'S GONE?!

BAM! BAM! BAM!

EEEEK! ANOTHER GHOST?!?

IT'S US! LET US OUT, SHAGGY!

LIKE, WHY'D YOU GO AND LOCK THE DOOR?

WE DIDN'T! IT'S STUCK! ARE YOU GONNA SAVE US OR WHAT?

SURE, SURE...

...BUT WHO'S GONNA S-S-SAVE ME?!?

EBENEZER... I AM THE GHOST OF CHRISTMAS PRESENT!

FOR M-M-ME? BUT I DIDN'T GET YOU ANYTHING!

C'MON, SHAGGY! LET US OUT ALREADY! WE'RE MISSING EVERYTHING!

WHA--?

CREE-EE-EAK!

WELL, HERE'S ONE THING WE DIDN'T MISS -- A TRAP DOOR AND SECRET PASSAGE!

IN MY CLOSET? I HAD NO IDEA! BUT WHERE DOES IT LEAD?

STRAIGHT TO YOUR *SHOP,* OF COURSE!

CRATCHET

WHY, THIS IS *CRATCHET'S* CUBICLE! HE MUST BE THE *CULPRIT!*

A REASONABLE *DEDUCTION.* CHECK OUT THIS BOX OF *"OFFICE SUPPLIES"* HE'S STASHED UNDER HIS DESK!

SPOOK SUITS! VELMA, I THINK WE'VE *FOUND* OUR *"GHOST!"*

LIKE, CAN THESE GHOSTS GET ANY *CREEPIER?* I DUNNO ABOUT *YOU,* SCOOB, BUT I SURE DON'T WANNA FIND OUT!

LET'S GET THIS DOOR *OPEN* BEFORE...

EBENEEZER...!

Y-Y-YOIKS!!

I AM THE GHOST OF CHRISTMAS *FUTURE...!*

G-G-GLAD TO MEET YOU! *WE* ARE THE GHOSTS OF CHRISTMAS *PAST--*

--LIKE, AS IN *"PAST TENSE!"* RUN FOR IT, SCOOBY-DOO!!

RI'M *RRRUNNING!* RI'M *RRRUNNING!*

SO BOB CRATCHET'S BEEN DRESSING UP AS THE *GHOSTS* INSTEAD OF *WORKING!* THAT'S WORSE THAN--

YAAHH!

...LYING DOWN ON THE JOB. UGH...!

THE JIG'S UP! WE'VE ADDED UP THE CLUES AND WE ALL KNOW YOU'RE *REALLY*...

...*TINY TIM?!?*

THAT'S RIGHT. I WANTED TO TEACH THE *OLD GOAT* A LESSON! HE TREATS GOOD PEOPLE LIKE MY FATHER LIKE *DIRT!* EVEN DURING *CHRISTMAS!*

IT'S TRUE. AND IF THAT'S WHAT YOU THINK, THEN ALL I CAN SAY IS...

...*MERRY CHRISTMAS!*

IS THIS CELEBRATION FOR *US?* MR. SCROOGE, YOU REALLY *HAVE* FOUND THE *CHRISTMAS SPIRIT!* THAT'S THE *BEST* PRESENT OF ALL!

NO--THE *BEST* PRESENT IS... I'M NOT *PRESSING* CHARGES!

HA HA HA HA

THE END

WHAT'S YOUR SCOOBY STYLE?

Which member of the gang are you most like? Take this groovy quiz to find out!

1. A phantom is causing trouble and your help is needed. What do you think?
A) It will be a challenge but I'm not afraid!
B) Like, get outta here! I don't want anything to do with a goony ghost!
C) Jeepers, that sounds exciting!
D) What a fascinating opportunity to find out more about a supernatural occurrence!

2. How would you describe your Scooby style?
A) You make a great leader
B) You're a laid-back dude
C) You're stylish and smart
D) You're a sensible brainbox

3. What essential tool do you carry in your mystery solving kit?
A) A Supernatural Sensor
B) A cushion to hide behind when a spook jumps out!
C) A camera
D) A spy glass

4. What's the most important skill a supersleuth needs?
A) The ability to create monster traps so those ghouls can't get away!
B) The ability to devour a super tower sandwich in three seconds flat!
C) Looking good when you catch those crooks!
D) If you can solve clues and crack codes, you will make an ace supersleuth!

5. What's your favourite colour?
A) Blue.
B) Brown
C) Purple
D) Orange

6. It's been a long day chasing ghosts and now you are ready for a monster snack! What do you choose?

A) A banana to keep your energy levels up
B) A supremo pizza with all the toppings
C) A healthy salad
D) A blueberry shake, cos blueberries are great for your brain power!

7. What's your favourite hobby?
A) Creating inventions
B) Snacking
C) Shopping
D) Reading detective novels

8. What's your favourite Scooby phrase?
A) That wraps up this mystery!
B) Zoinks!
C) Jeepers
D) Jinkies

HOW DID YOU DOO?

MOSTLY A'S
You and Fred would make a great mystery solving duo! You both love a good mystery and you can use your detective skills to get to the bottom of any crime. Fred is seriously impressed by your top sleuthing skills!

MOSTLY B'S
Scooby and Shaggy reckon you totally rock! Mysteries are so not the way to go for you, cos you hate all things spooky! You'd much rather kick back with a pizza and leave the spooky stuff to Velma and the gang!

MOSTLY C'S
Just like Daphne, you enjoy solving mysteries, even though you can get a bit spooked sometimes. You both have a great sense of style and love to get into the Scooby groove!

MOSTLY D'S
You love nothing more than cracking a mind-boggling mystery! Just like Velma, you are top of the class when it comes to mystery solving and your brain power never fails you. You've got just what it takes to join the gang!

ICY
RECEPTION

FRANK STROM -- writer
ANTHONY WILLIAMS -- penciller * JEFF ALBRECHT -- inker
TOM ORZECHOWSKI -- letterer * PAUL BECTON -- colorist
DIGITAL CHAMELEON -- separations

FATHER FROST AND HIS "GHOSTS" WILL BE LOOKING FOR YOU IN THE CITY. BUT NO ONE WILL EVER FIND YOU...

...HERE!

A COUNTRY SNOW LODGE! FREDDY, YOU'RE A GENIUS!

HIM? I THOUGHT OF IT-- HE'S JUST ALONG TO DRIVE THE VAN!

OH, VELMA-- THIS PLACE IS BEAUTIFUL!

AND COMPLETELY SECURE! BUT JUST IN CASE, WE'LL BE GUARDING YOU NIGHT AND DAY. WE'LL NEVER GOOF OFF OR...

GANGWAY! COMIN' THROUGH! COWABUNGA!

STOP!!!

SCREEEECH!!

YOU'RE NOT GOING ANYWHERE, SHAGGY.

YEAH, SOMEBODY'S GOT TO GUARD NATASHA WHILE WE QUESTION THE SUSPECTS!

OH, MAN! NO FUN!

CONTINUED ON PAGE 42

SCOOBY SNACKS!

Prepare to snack like the scoobster with the official Scooby Snacks recipe! Mm-mm!

WHAT YOU NEED!

1 cup of brown sugar,
3/4 cup of desiccated coconut,
1/2 cup of flour,
1/4 cup of of butter,
1 egg,
1 teaspoon of vanilla essence,
1 teaspoon of baking powder.

WHAT TO DOO!

1. Melt the butter and sugar in a saucepan.
2. Leave the mixture to cool, add the vanilla essence and the egg and mix together.
3. Sieve the flour and baking powder into a bowl.
4. Pour the butter mixture into the bowl and add the desiccated coconut. Stir together.
5. Place spoonfuls of the mixture onto a baking sheet and press into a diamond shape, so they look like Scooby's dog tag!
6. Bake at 180˚ or gas mark 4 for 6 minutes or until they are golden.
7. Let them cool and they are ready to eat! You could even decorate them with yellow icing to look like Scooby's tag!

SHAGGY SHAKE!

Wash your Scooby Snacks down with a delicious Shaggy Shake!

WHAT YOU NEED!

3 ripe bananas,
300ml tub of vanilla ice cream,
Milk.

WHAT TO DOO!

1. Peel the bananas and break them into chunks.
2. Put them in a blender and pour in enough milk to come half-way up the banana chunks.
3. Add the ice-cream and give it a blitz! Pour the shake into a glass, and serve with a whole lotta Scooby Snacks!

PUPPET POWER!

Zoinks, check out these groovy Scooby and Shaggy puppets! They're, like, so handy man! Follow these easy steps and make them for yourself!

Draw the outline of your puppet onto paper. Check that your hand fits inside the shape. Cut it out, and lay it onto the brown felt. Cut out two of these shapes from the brown felt.

Spread a thin line of glue around the outside of one of the shapes, (but not along the bottom!) and place the other felt shape on top to make your basic puppet.

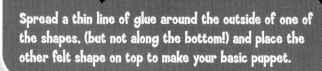

Add the Scooby details – cut a piece of brown felt for his muzzle, black for his nose and mouth, red for his tongue and blue and yellow for his collar. Cut white circles for eyes. Position the pieces on the puppet and then glue them into position.

AND SO...

OF *COURSE* I *RESENT* KRYLOVA'S CHOICE OF AN AMERICAN TRAINER! IT'S A SLAP IN THE FACE TO OUR RUSSIAN HERITAGE!

AND AS AN OFFICIAL OF THE *FEDERATION*, MIGHT YOU...?

NYET! HER ACTIONS *DISPLEASE* US, BUT SHE *STILL* REPRESENTS OUR *NATIONAL SKATING CLUB.* SO AS YOU CAN SEE, I HAVE NO *MOTIVE.*

HOWEVER, THE SAME CANNOT BE SAID OF HER *FORMER* COACH!

SURE--YOU MUST BE *UPSET* THAT NATASHA *FIRED* YOU, MRS. PETROVA!

YES, OF COURSE. BUT YOU DON'T UNDERSTAND--

--I COULD NEVER HOLD A *GRUDGE* UNDER THESE CIRCUMSTANCES.

HER NEW COACH, *MR. CARROLL,* IS A DEAR OLD *FRIEND*... AND NATASHA IS LIKE A *DAUGHTER* TO ME. I DON'T *HATE* HER!

THAT'S RIGHT-- I *HATE* HER.

AHA!!! SO YOU *ADMIT* IT!

DA. IS NO BIG SECRET.

OH, I DIDN'T *ALWAYS* HATE HER. SHE WAS SO *CUTE* AS A CHILD WITH HER LITTLE *APPLE CHEEKS.* AND SHE COULD *SPIN* LIKE A *TOP!* I THOUGHT SHE WAS *ADORABLE...*

...BUT THEN SHE STARTED *BEATING ME,* THE LITTLE *PEASANT!!* I COULD KILL HER!

ER...IS JUST *FIGURE OF SPEECH,* DOLLINK. YOU'RE NOT GOING TO *POLICE?*

NO, NO-- I JUST WANT A LOOK AT THE *TV EQUIPMENT.*

HMM. CAMERAS... MICROPHONES-- NOTHING OUT OF THE ORDINARY.

EXCEPT... ONE PIECE OF EQUIPMENT IS *MISSING!*

THAT'S IT!!

YOW! WATCH WHERE YOU'RE GOING, SHAGGY! WHAT GIVES?

G-G-GHOSTS! THE ICE IS FULL OF 'EM!!

CALM DOWN. THEY'RE GONE-- VANISHED WITHOUT A TRACE.

OH, THEY LEFT A TRACE, ALL RIGHT. THESE IMPRESSIONS IN THE SNOW LOOK LIKE THEY WERE MADE BY A CAMERA TRIPOD...

...AND THAT PROVES MY THEORY!

THESE "GHOSTS" CAN'T HURT YOU, SHAGGY--THEY'RE PROJECTIONS.

WHOEVER IS BEHIND THIS IS USING STOLEN LIGHTING EQUIPMENT FROM THE ARENA TO PROJECT "GHOSTS" ONTO THE ICE!

≷WHEW!≶ THAT'S GREAT, BUT WHO WOULD WANT TO SCARE NATASHA? FATHER FROST?

NOBODY'S ACTUALLY SEEN FATHER FROST. MARIA ROTTENOVA IS THE MOST LIKELY CULPRIT-- SHE'S GOT THE MOTIVE, AND NOTHING TO LOSE!

WHY, THAT'S TERRIBLE!

NO--THAT'S TERRIFIC! NOW THAT I KNOW THE GHOSTS ARE FAKE, NOTHING CAN STOP ME FROM WINNING THE COMPETITION!

AND SO...

NO SIGN OF MARIA OR FATHER FROST ANYWHERE!

BAD LUCK FOR THEM-- THEY'RE GONNA MISS NATASHA SKATING HER WAY TO A GOLD MEDAL!

DOO YOU KNOW?

So you think you know everything about Scooby and his supersleuth sidekicks? Find out with this cool quiz!

1. Which member of the gang wears an orange ascot tie?

2. Which of these is a Scooby villain?
a) Greenbeard the pirate
b) Redbeard the pirate

3. Who do these ears belong to?

4. Which member of the gang says 'JINKIES!'?

5. True or false - Shaggy's real name is Norman? ☐ T ☐ F

6. Velma has lost her glasses, can you work out what she is looking at?

7. What breed of dog is Scooby?

8. What does Fred say when the gang solve a mystery?
A) Scooby-dooby-doo!
B) That sorted that monster out!
C) That wraps up this mystery!

9. What is the name of the town where the gang are from?
A) Coolsville   B) Spookyville

10. Who is the oldest member of the gang?

A) Fred   B) Velma

11. True or false - Scooby is afraid of his own shadow?

12. What shape is Scooby's dog tag?

48

How to be a Supersleuth!

Fred reveals some of the gang's secrets for being a tip-top supersleuth!

PERFECT PRINTS

Fingerprints are a vital clue used by all ace detectives! A fingerprint is the pattern on the end of your fingers. When you touch a surface, the oils on your skin leave a print.

Fingerprints are usually invisible but detectives dust a special powder over a surface to reveal them.

No two fingerprints are identical so they are a great way to identify a crook. Velma is an expert at finger printing and has used it to solve many Mystery, Inc. cases!

RECORD YOUR FINGER PRINTS!

1. Draw a circle on a piece of paper and colour it in with a pencil.
2. Press your finger in the circle to cover your finger tip in pencil.
3. Press your finger against a piece of sticky tape.
4. Hold the tape against some white paper and your fingerprint will be revealed!

I SPY!

A magnifying glass, is a vital piece of mystery-solving equipment! Also known as a spy glass, it is the best way to search for clues and examine evidence in detail. Test your spy glass skills – can you work out what Fred is looking at through these magnifying glasses?

A) B) C)

REST IN PIZZA

STARLIGHT MOTEL

OKAY, GANG, LET'S GO OVER THE *CLUES* WE'VE FOUND ONE MORE TIME...

GOOD IDEA, FREDDIE. THERE ARE *SO MANY*, IT'S HARD TO KEEP THEM ALL STRAIGHT!

COULDN'T WE DO THIS *AFTER* DINNER? LIKE, WE'RE *STARVING* OVER HERE!

REAH! RUNGRY!

JOHN ROZUM-WRITER
KAREN MATCHETTE- PENCILLER
DAVE HUNT- INKER
RYAN CLINE- LETTERER
PAUL BECTON- COLORIST
HARVEY RICHARDS- ASST. EDITOR
JOAN HILTY- EDITOR

WE'RE STARTING TO MAKE SOME REAL PROGRESS HERE, SHAGGY. IF YOU AND SCOOBY ARE THAT HUNGRY, WHY DON'T YOU ORDER A *PIZZA?*

HMMM...NOW WHERE DOES THE *THREE-FINGERED GLOVE* FIT INTO ALL OF THIS?

PIZZA! WHAT A *GREAT IDEA!*

WHAT ABOUT *THIS?*

I'M PRETTY SURE THAT MASK DOESN'T HAVE ANYTHING TO DO WITH THIS CASE, DAPHNE.

PAUKSDS21

HELLO? PARCHEESIE PIZZA? I'D LIKE TO ORDER FIVE LARGE PIZZAS WITH THE WORKS. WE'RE AT THE STARLIGHT MOTEL IN ROOM 105.

DO YOU GUARANTEE DELIVERY IN 30 MINUTES OR LESS? PERFECT, 'CAUSE WE'RE *STARVING* HERE!

THANKS, SHAGGY--THAT WAS NICE OF YOU TO ORDER US PIZZAS AS WELL.

HUH? YOU WANTED PIZZA? I GUESS YOU'LL HAVE TO CALL THEM BACK. I BARELY ORDERED ENOUGH FOR ME AND SCOOB!

OKAY, IT'S SEVEN O'CLOCK NOW, THAT MEANS THE PIZZAS SHOULD BE HERE BY SEVEN-THIRTY.

HERE WE GO!

REAH! REAH!

7:35!

THE PIZZAS AREN'T HERE! WHAT ARE WE GONNA DO, SCOOB? WE'LL STARVE!

ROH, NO!

WILL YOU TWO CLOWNS CALM DOWN! THE PIZZA DELIVERY PERSON IS PROBABLY JUST TRYING TO FIND OUR ROOM, THAT'S ALL.

MAYBE YOU'RE RIGHT, BUT...

I DON'T SEE ANYONE!

FRED, DAPHNE, THIS IS NO TIME FOR SITTING AROUND, THERE'S A MYSTERY TO BE SOLVED--

--THE MYSTERY OF THE MISSING PIZZAS!

YOUR STOMACH WILL JUST HAVE TO WAIT IN LINE. IN CASE YOU'VE FORGOTTEN, WE ALREADY HAVE A MYSTERY TO SOLVE--

--THE MYSTERY OF THE VANISHING VENTRILOQUIST!

WELL, THEN, SCOOB...IT LOOKS LIKE IT'S UP TO US!

ROU CAN CROUNT ON ME, RAGGY!

I JUST HOPE WE CAN FIND THOSE PIZZAS BEFORE THEY GET COLD.

105

CONTINUED ON PAGE 56

Groovyscopes!

AQUARIUS (JAN 21 – FEB 19)

Shaggy says: Like, you've got a totally exciting time ahead, isn't that right Scoob? It's like, a fab time to try new things, maybe a new sandwich filling? May I suggest cheese, piccalilli and raspberry relish? Mm-mm!

PISCES (FEB 20 – MAR 20)

Daphne says: Jeepers, this is a fabulous time for you to update your wardrobe! You have a great sense of style, and you love to look good. Beware of werewolves on the next full moon, they sure give me the shivers!

ARIES (MAR 21 – APR 20)

Fred says: Arians make great team leaders and that's a great skill to have! Make the most of it and don't be afraid to take the lead. Don't worry about making tricky decisions, that's exactly what you're good at!

TAURUS (APR 21 – MAY 21)

Velma says: Hmmm. You've got a mystery to solve. Use your brain power, logic and top detective skills and this mini mystery won't be a problem for you. Good luck, I will be interested to hear how you get on!

GEMINI (MAY 22 – JUN 22)

Shaggy says: Like, beware of hairy scary things cos you never know where they are hiding. Like, you gotta avoid all things mysterious, they are waaay too much trouble. Chow down with a pizza instead!

CANCER (JUN 23 – JUL 23)

Daphne: You have a choice to make. If, like me, you make the wrong choice and fall through a trap door, landing in the arms of a zombie, remember what to do: scream "AAIIIIEEE!" as loudly as you can and wait for your friends to come and rescue you!

LEO (JUL 24 – AUG 23)

Fred says: Leos are as brave as lions and that's just what you need for monster hunting! Don't be afraid to ask for help, you may think you can cope on your own but it's always good to have friends to back you up!

VIRGO (AUG 24 – SEP 23)

Velma says: This is a great time to take up a new hobby. It's an excellent way to expand the mind. How about a 'Dusting for Fingerprints' course, or Algebraphysiology. Both are fascinating and very useful.

LIBRA (SEP 24 – OCT 23)

Shaggy says: Get into the Scooby groove and, like, totally chill out! Kick back with a banoffee burger and enjoy a little bit of you time. And if anyone says the word 'mystery', just pretend you haven't heard them.

SCORPIO (OCT 24 – NOV 22)

Daphne says: Look out for spooky fog and mist patches, because it always spells trouble. Not only does it mean that Redbeard the Pirate is about to cross your path, but fog also plays havoc with your hairdo!

SAGITTARIUS (NOV 23 – DEC 21)

Fred says: The year ahead looks awesome for you! Watch out around Hallowe'en as you may attract some trouble from The Creeper but don't worry, give Mystery, Inc. a call and we'll sort that bad guy out for you!

CAPRICORN (DEC 22 – JAN 20)

REAT ROTS OF ROOBY RACKS AND ROOK OUT FOR RHOSTS! REE-HEE-HEE! ROOBY-ROOBY -ROOOO!

55

CONTINUED FROM PAGE 54

ARE YOU OKAY?

YEAH, MAN, I THINK SO...

LIKE, YOU WOULDN'T HAVE BEEN DELIVERING PIZZAS TO THE *STARLIGHT MOTEL*, WOULD YOU?

YEAH, WHY, ARE YOU THE GUY WHO ORDERED 'EM?

SORRY, DUDE, BUT LIKE THE MONSTER TOOK 'EM. CONKED ME ON THE HEAD, AND RAN OFF WITH ALL FIVE PIES.

MAN, I'M GOING TO GO SEE IF ANYONE'S HIRING AT THE MALL. I AIN'T DOING THIS JOB ANYMORE!

WELL, SCOOB, THERE GOES OUR FIRST CLUE!

HOOT-HOOT HOOT-HOOT

ZOINKS! WHAT'S *THAT*?

OH {HEH-HEH} IT'S JUST AN OWL.

GROIINK GROIINK

RAT'S NO ROWL!

NO, BUT IT'S JUST A FROG.

GRROOOAARR

AROTHER FROG?!

MAYBE THAT'S A *LI'L BUNNY*...

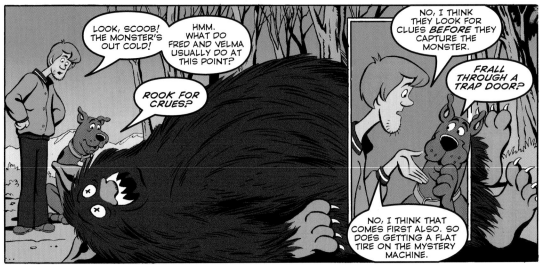

OH, THE **MONSTER'S** MASK!

THERE. THAT DOESN'T HELP-- I STILL DON'T KNOW WHO THIS GUY IS.

OOOOG...

RHEE REITHER.

LOOK, I...

ALL I KNOW IS HE REALLY LIKES PIZZA.

I'LL TELL YOU, ALREADY! I'M PAUL PASSOLINI. MY FATHER OWNS "PASSOLINI'S PIZZA," WHICH HAS BEEN AROUND FOR OVER FORTY YEARS--

--UP UNTIL THAT *PARCHEESIE PIZZA* CHAIN OPENED ITS DOORS AND STARTED STEALING HIS BUSINESS WITH ITS TERRIBLE PIZZA AND SPEEDING DRIVERS!

PARCHEESIE PIZZA DOESN'T CARE ABOUT PIZZA, THEY JUST CARE ABOUT **MONEY**.

I WAS TRYING TO CAUSE TROUBLE FOR PARCHEESIE SO THEY'D LEAVE TOWN. THEN MY FATHER'S BUSINESS WOULD BE SAVED.

NOW YOU TWO HAVE RUINED *EVERYTHING!*

NOT YET, BUT DON'T WORRY, WE WILL--

--FOR *PARCHEESIE PIZZA!*

I'LL NEED YOUR **MONSTER COSTUME.**

MYSTERY SOLVED!

THANKS FOR ALL YOUR HELP!

HONORARY
MYSTERY, INC. MEMBER...

NAME: